ANIMALS UNDER THREAT

ASIAN ELEPHANT

IN DANGER OF EXTINCTION!

Matt Turner

Heinemann
LIBRARY

www.heinemann.co.uk/library
Visit our website to find out more information about **Heinemann Library** books.

To order:
☎ Phone 44 (0) 1865 888066
▤ Send a fax to 44 (0) 1865 314091
▦ Visit the Heinemann Bookshop at www.heinemann.co.uk/library to browse our catalogue and order online.

First published in Great Britain by Heinemann Library, Halley Court, Jordan Hill, Oxford OX2 8EJ, part of Harcourt Education. Heinemann is a registered trademark of Harcourt Education Ltd.

Editorial: Gianna Quaglia, Nicole Irving and Louise Galpine
Design: Rob Norridge and Jo Malivoire
Picture Research: Laura Durman
Illustrations: Stefan Chabluk and Stuart Lafford
Production: Camilla Smith

Originated by Dot Gradations Ltd
Printed in China by WKT Company Limited

ISBN 0 431 18902 1
09 08 07 06 05
10 9 8 7 6 5 4 3 2 1

British Library Cataloguing in Publication Data
Turner, Matt
Asian elephant - (Animals under threat)
599.6'76
A full catalogue record for this book is available from the British Library.

Acknowledgements

The publishers would like to thank the following for permission to reproduce photographs: Alamy pp. **7** (C. Fredriksson), **41** (D. Simpson); ardea.com pp. **16**, **21** (J. Rajput), **18**, **25**, **40** (J. Van Gruisen), **27** (P. Cavendish), **36** (T. & P. Leeson); Bruce Coleman p. **17** (J. P. Zwaenepoel); FLPA pp. **5** (D. Hosking), **13**, **20** (Silvestris), **28** (K. Rushford), **31** (G. Marcoaldi), **34** (M. Newman); Gerald Cubitt pp. **9**, **10**, **38**, **43**; NHPA pp. **12** (N. Garbutt), **14** (K. Schafer), **30** (A. & S. Toon), **35** (E. Janes), **39** (D. Heuclin); OSF pp. **22** (V. Sinha), **29** (A. Desai); Still pp. **15**, **23**, **24** (R. Seitre), **26** (M. Edwards), **32** (J. Etchart), **33** (M. Gunther); www.thetravelstory.com p. **11** (P. S. Kristensen). Special thanks to IFAW for the image on page **42**.

Cover photograph reproduced with permission of Mary Plage (OSF) and Photodisc.

The publishers would like to thank Michael Chinery for his assistance in the preparation of this book.

Contents

Words printed in the text in bold, **like this**, are explained in the Glossary.

The Asian elephant

The Asian elephant is one of nature's giants. The largest can weigh as much as 70 adult humans, or up to 6 tons. The world's second-largest land animal, only the African elephant is bigger.

Asian and African elephants are **mammals**. They are actually two separate **species**, which means that they cannot **breed** together and produce offspring. As well as being smaller and lighter than the African elephant, the Asian elephant also has more toenails on its hindfeet, one fewer pair of ribs and a greater number of bones in its back.

All species have a scientific name. The African elephant is known as *Loxodonta africana*, while the Asian elephant is called *Elephas maximus*. Scientists divide the Asian elephant population into five subspecies. These are *Elephas maximus maximus* (found in Sri Lanka), *Elephas maximus indicus* (found in India and South-east Asia), *Elephas maximus sumatranus* (from Sumatra) and *Elephas maximus hirsutus* on the Malay **peninsula**. A fifth subspecies, the pygmy elephant of Borneo, has only recently been reported and is not yet named. There are only small differences between the subspecies. *Elephas maximus hirsutus* is hairier than the others. The pygmy elephant is the smallest; it has straighter tusks and larger ears, and its tail is longer compared to its body size.

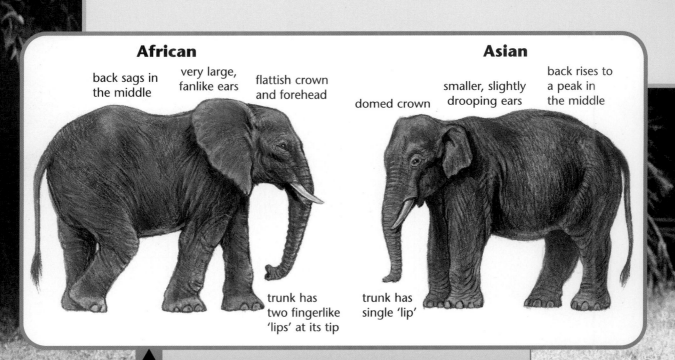

African

back sags in the middle

very large, fanlike ears

flattish crown and forehead

trunk has two fingerlike 'lips' at its tip

Asian

domed crown

smaller, slightly drooping ears

back rises to a peak in the middle

trunk has single 'lip'

At a glance the two species of elephant might look the same, but there are key differences to look out for.

In its cousin's shadow

Though both elephant species have grown rarer over the years, attention has focused mostly on the African elephant, which has been heavily hunted for its **ivory** tusks. In comparison, the Asian elephant has been largely ignored. There are huge numbers of Asian elephants in captivity, so people tend to assume that they are not endangered. But in the wild they are running out of space as people take over or change the elephants' natural **habitat**. If the world does not take steps to save it, the Asian elephant will quietly vanish from the wild.

An Asian elephant – not as famous as its African cousin, but also endangered.

Yesterday's giants

There are just two elephant species alive today, but once there were many. Their earliest ancestors lived in what is now south Asia and Africa, and spread to every continent on Earth except Antarctica and Australasia. There were many different forms of elephant: some had shovel-like jaws, others had peg-like tusks.

Mammoths were long-tusked cousins of modern elephants. Some were huge, standing over one metre taller than a modern Asian elephant. The woolly mammoth lived in the treeless north of the North American continent, Europe and Asia. It had a shaggy coat to keep out cold weather and biting insects, and it probably fed on mosses and shrubs. We know what woolly mammoths looked like because their remains have been found, perfectly preserved, in ice. Mammoths died out about 10,000 years ago. Changes in climate and plant life may have killed them off, though by that date humans were already hunting mammoths for their meat.

Asian elephant distribution

The Asian elephant once ranged over a vast area of Asia. It was found from Syria and Iraq in the west to Borneo in the east, and from the island of Sumatra in the south to at least as far north as China's Yangtze (Chang Jiang) River. By AD 1000, the elephant had vanished from Syria, Iraq, Java and most of southern China.

The Asian elephant is now found in thirteen countries: India, Nepal, Bangladesh, Bhutan, Sri Lanka, Myanmar (Burma), Thailand, Malaysia, Indonesia, Laos, Cambodia, Vietnam and China. India, Sri Lanka, Bhutan, Nepal and Bangladesh contain over 60 per cent of all Asia's wild elephants. Cambodia, China, Laos and Vietnam together account for less than 5 per cent.

PAKISTAN
NEPAL BHUTAN
BANGLADESH
CHINA
TAIWAN
INDIA
MYANMAR LAOS
N
Bay of
Bengal
THAILAND
CAMBODIA
VIETNAM
South
China
Sea
PHILIPPINES
SRI
LANKA
INDIAN
OCEAN
BRUNEI
Celebes
Sea
MALAYSIA
0   1000
kilometres
Borneo
Sumatra INDONESIA

■ Elephant distribution today

Scattered blocks are all that remain of the elephant's range across mainland and island Asia.

Broken distribution

If you gathered together all the plots of land occupied by Asian elephants, you would end up with a total area of nearly 500,000 square kilometres. This is an area a little smaller than France. Before large-scale human settlements began to develop in India around 3000 BC, the elephant had a stable population on the mainland. Today, as the map shows, this population is broken up into separate pieces.

Elephants have vanished completely from central India. In the rest of India, elephant numbers are down to 25,000 in all the interior and northwestern states. Their largest populations are scattered about the hill regions of the south-west (9600–15,200 animals) and the north-east (about 6800 animals). Small populations are strung out in blocks along the Himalayan foothills. In Myanmar and Thailand, populations are similarly scattered. Each block is itself broken down into many tiny, separate portions.

Chinese elephants

In ancient China, most peasant farmers looked on elephants as a threat to their land and their crops. A ruler in 1105 BC is said to have driven away 'the tiger, leopard, rhinoceros and elephant to the great joy of the people'. As they cleared the ancient forests and planted crops, over thousands of years, Chinese peasants stead ly pushed elephants southwards. Today, China's elephants are reduced to about 300 individuals in the southern province of Yunnan.

Human help

In rare cases, human acts have helped spread the Asian elephant's population. In the Andaman Islands in the Bay of Bengal, between 20 and 30 elephants survive from a tiny population introduced there as working animals in the **logging** industry.

The pygmy elephant was trapped on the island of Borneo when sea levels rose long ago. As time passed, its appearance and behaviour changed, and it is now different from other kinds of elephant.

A new elephant

In September 2003 scientists analysing elephant **DNA** announced that Borneo's elephants are a separate subspecies of Asian elephant. It had once been thought that the island's elephants had died out in **prehistoric** times, and the current population was descended from elephants given as a present to a local ruler in 1750. This has been proved wrong. Scientists now say that the elephants have been cut off from other Asian populations for about 300,000 years. During this time they have evolved into a different elephant – one that is smaller and less aggressive.

How many Asian elephants?

The total population of Asian elephants that lived in the wild in 1900 is thought to have been 100,000. Today there are between 34,500 and 51,000, though most researchers think the true figure is a high average of these figures: about 45,000–48,000. There are another 16,000 or so elephants in captivity. This is a tiny fraction of the total numbers that have been captured throughout recorded history: an estimated two to four million elephants, including about 100,000 just in the past hundred years.

Population totals are falling throughout Asia, but the rate of decline varies from one region to another. Some of the hardest-hit regions are in south-east Asia. One 2002 report revealed that, since 1990, elephant numbers have dropped by more than 90 per cent in Vietnam, by nearly 90 per cent in Cambodia, and by 50 per cent in Laos, a nation once known as the 'Land of a Million Elephants'. In Thailand, within the past 20 years, the elephant popuation may have declined by 50 per cent.

Population chart

These figures show the approximate minimum, maximum and probable Asian elephant population counts for each region.

Region	Minimum number of elephants	Probable number of elephants	Maximum number of elephants
India	19,100	24,300	29,450
Nepal	40	50	60
Bangladesh	200	220	240
Bhutan	60	80	100
Sri Lanka	3200	3800	4400
Myanmar	4600	4800	5000
Thailand	1300	1700	2000
Malaysia	800	1000	1200
Borneo	1000	1300	1500
Indonesia	2800	3800	4800
Laos	1000	1100	1300
Cambodia	200	250	500
Vietnam	100	140	145
China	250	280	300
Total	**34,650**	**42,820**	**50,995**

Islands of elephants

The breaking-up of its population is one of the most serious threats facing the elephant today. Human settlements form barriers that split elephant country into fragments. Elephant populations are divided into small groups that cannot mix with one another. Adult elephants find it increasingly hard to find a **mate** at **breeding** time.

Below a certain figure, the long-term chance of survival for any animal **species** falls. Scientists put this figure at about 500 individuals. Any smaller, and a population starts to lose its **genetic diversity**. If the animals in a group are closely related, they can all fall ill from the same thing. A small population can easily be wiped out by disease.

Complicated counting

Scientists are unsure of how many elephants there actually are because elephants are surprisingly hard to count! They are easily hidden in the forests where they live. Also, many populations live on national borders where political problems make it difficult to mount joint surveys. So field researchers have to be inventive. To avoid counting the same animal twice, they look for odd features, such as broken or twisted tusks, or torn ears. To be able to tell one elephant from another they also look at size. Researchers can calculate an animal's height from a photograph. Footprints are useful, too: an elephant's shoulder height is approximately twice the **circumference** of its forefoot. Another method involves measuring the volume of dung in a given area. It is messy but very helpful, since the dung is also used in other scientific tests.

There's no mistaking this individual: it has only one tusk. Special features like this help researchers count elephant populations accurately.

Asian elephant country

The Asian elephant can survive almost anywhere so long as there are trees to give shelter from the hot sun. It is at home in marshes, bamboo forests, palm tree **thickets** and grassy **scrub**. It is even found in the Himalayan foothills, where it withstands the freezing night-time temperatures.

The densest elephant populations are found in dry, thorny scrub forest where there is a single annual **monsoon** (wet season) giving 600–2000 millimetres of rainfall. Dry scrub forest is common in southern India and Sri Lanka.

Tropical rainforest covers much of south-east Asia, including most of the Malay **peninsula**. Undisturbed rainforest contains surprisingly few elephants. It is too **humid**, and food plants are too widely scattered. Rainforest that has been opened up a little by humans, but not destroyed, is better. It contains regular sunlit clearings where food plants for elephants can grow.

River deep, mountain high

Elephants must drink plenty and often, so they need to live near a good source of water. The **floodplains** of major Asian rivers as well as countless smaller waterways, once swarmed with elephants.

Elephants need water. This lake in south-west India was created in 1895 to provide hunting grounds for the British, but today it lies at the heart of a wildlife sanctuary.

Unfortunately, an elephant's ideal home is similar to ours. The first places humans settled in Asia were fertile, wooded and grassy floodplains. In due course people pushed the elephants out. Today, elephants are concentrated mostly in hilly regions, such as the Western and Eastern Ghats of southern India, the Dangreks on the Thailand/Cambodia border, and the Cardamom and Elephant Mountains in Cambodia. Hill ranges are typically the last types of terrain to be settled or cultivated by people.

Home on the range

Elephants are constantly on the move from one day to the next, and from one season to another, in search of food, water, shelter or each other. The area of land to which each elephant herd keeps, and which contains all the elephants' needs, is called a **home range**. The size of a home range varies hugely, depending on whether **resources** are widely scattered or not, and whether the animals are free to roam or are hemmed in by dams, villages and crops. The range may measure from 20 square kilometres up to 600 square kilometres. It varies in size depending on the time of year, and may treble in size during the dry season. Regularly used forests become laced with elephant paths and dotted with clearings in which they gather.

Measuring range

Space technology helps us measure elephant ranges, through use of the global positioning system (GPS). Researchers fit **radio transmitters** to **tranquillized** elephants that are then released back into the wild. The transmitter sends a signal to a **satellite** in space, which beams the signal back to a receiver and computer on Earth showing exactly where the animal is. The researchers use the GPS data to calculate how far each individual elephant roams. By tracking several different elephants they can monitor seasonal movements and calculate an average home range figure.

Asian elephant bodies

Asian elephants are true giants. In a standing pose, the body's great weight is slung like a bridge between the fore and hind limbs, which have thick bones and act like sturdy pillars. The limb joints are arranged for bearing loads, not for running fast. The elephant usually walks at about 3–4 kilometres per hour, though it can charge at up to 40 kilometres per hour. It is the only land mammal that cannot jump.

Body basics

An elephant's trunk is really an elongated upper lip and nose with the two nostrils at its tip, but it has an incredible range of uses. It can function as a hand for picking up seeds, tearing out trees or touching another elephant tenderly. It can sniff the air for distant scents or deliver a wide range of calls. It is also a 'hosepipe' for sucking up and squirting out water.

Teeth and tusks

An elephant's tusks are overgrown teeth. The '**ivory**' is a dense, hard, creamy-white material called dentine. Bulls, or male elephants, have long tusks, while cows, or female elephants, have stubby, down-curving tusks known as tushes. Not all bulls have tusks. Whether they do or not depends partly on where they live. In Cambodia, almost none have tusks, while in southern India over 90 per cent do. Overall, one in ten Asian elephants (male and female) have tusks.

*The male Asian elephant, or bull, has much longer tusks than the female. Heavy **poaching**, which continues to this day, means that magnificent tusks like these are now rarely seen.*

An elephant has 24 back teeth during its lifetime. As the teeth wear out they break up, and others slowly move forward to replace them. By the age of 30 to 40 the elephant is using its final, sixth set of **molars**: great, brick-sized teeth that weigh up to 3.5 kilograms each. When these go, at about 50 to 60 years of age, the elephant starves to death because it cannot chew its food.

An elephant's trunk, which can hold several litres of water, is useful for soaking the skin as well as for drinking.

Air supply

An elephant needs plenty of oxygen to fuel its huge body. People think that oxygen starvation is a common cause of death in captive elephants. The harder a body works, the more oxygen it needs in its blood. The elephant's heart muscles take in oxygen quite slowly. If an elephant is overworked, its heart simply does not get enough oxygen to keep up.

Keeping cool

Losing body heat is extremely important to an elephant, but it has no sweat **glands**. Provided its skin stays wet, water will **evaporate** from it, taking body heat away. That is why an elephant likes to wallow in rivers or slap on a wet 'mudpack'. When there is no water available, it may use its trunk to suck moisture from its mouth and spray this over its skin. In ideal conditions about 4–5 litres of water evaporate from an adult's body every hour. An elephant also uses its ears to stay cool. The body's heat is carried to a network of blood vessels lining the ears. The elephant flaps its ears to make air currents that draw the heat away. In a breeze, the elephant simply sticks its ears straight out.

Size basics

Head and body length (including tusks)	5.4–6.4 metres	
Tail length	1.2–1.5 metres	
Shoulder height	2.5–3 metres (females 25% smaller)	
Average weight bull	5.4 metric tons	
cow	2.7 metric tons	

Silent step

Despite its size an elephant can move incredibly quietly. Its weight is spread over a large area. An elephant's 'total footprint' (the area of ground covered by all four soles) is about a square metre. Beneath the elephant's foot bones are thick soles of fat that act like cushions, muffling the cracking of sticks. Each sole spreads out under the weight, then shrinks again on lifting, so the feet do not get stuck in mud.

Food and feeding

Elephants are vegetarians. They eat a mixed diet of grasses and **browse** (the name for the leaves, woody twigs and bark from trees and shrubs). They also eat fruits, flowers and roots. Increasingly, elephants feed on planted crops, and this is a serious cause of conflict with farmers.

Varying diet

Across their range, Asian elephants select from as many as 400 different plant **species**. What they eat, and when they eat it, varies from one region to another. In a study in southern India, browse made up 70 per cent of the elephants' diet during the January–April dry season. In the heavy May–June rains, the elephants ate fresh grasses, which made up 54 per cent of their diet. As the diet changed, so the elephants moved from one food source to another. During the rainy months they spread out into grassy areas. In dry months they clustered in river valleys.

Daily dining

Elephants have giant appetites. An adult usually eats over 100 kilograms of food per day, but can eat three times that if hungry. To take in its mighty meals the elephant must feed morning, afternoon and night for about 14 hours in every 24. Usually it rests in the midday heat. All that fodder means gas – lots of it. An elephant produces almost 2000 litres of gas each day, enough to keep a living-room gas fire burning for ten hours!

Asian elephants browse on tree parts. Some trees die as a result, but others are stimulated into sending out new growth.

Packing its trunk

The Asian elephant uses its trunk to collect food and pass it to its mouth. It curls the trunk around long grasses and rips them up. It may use its forefeet to hold **vegetation** down while ripping and to kick and loosen tussocks of grass. To strip bark from branches, an elephant uses its trunk tip to twist the branch against its teeth. To pick up fruits and seeds from the ground, the elephant delicately dabs each on to the tip of its trunk.

The Asian elephant is a thirsty drinker, drinking about 90 litres of water a day. The elephant's trunk can hold five to six litres of water in one go. It usually drinks every day at least once, but can go several days without water if necessary. Elephants are experts at finding hidden water. In long dry spells they kick at dried-up riverbeds, allowing groundwater to well up into the holes they dig. They can smell rain from several kilometres' distance.

Help with digestion

Almost half of an elephant's food passes straight through the **gut** and into the dung, without being **digested** at all. This is because the elephant's gut, where digestion takes place, is relatively short. Help, however, is given by tiny **organisms** called microbes. They live in the elephant's gut and help break down the food (which also nourishes the microbes).

Seed sowers

Elephants don't just take food; they help to grow it too. When they eat plant seeds, they often pass undigested through the elephant's warm gut. By the time they are passed out again in dung, the hard seed cases are usually softened. The softening and warmth encourage the seed to **germinate** quickly. By moving a seed from the shade of its 'parent' tree to another part of forest, an elephant also helps spread its food plants about.

Asian elephant groups

Elephants are social animals that live in herds. This habit helps young elephants learn essential survival skills from their elders.

Strong bond

The bond between a cow (female) and her young is so strong that calves stay close to their mother even into their teens. Cow–calf units form the basic building blocks of herds, which today usually number 15–40 animals. The cows are fiercely protective of their young and form a defensive ring around them if threatened by danger. In fact, adult elephants' only **predators** are people, though tigers may attack calves.

Cows grow up and stay in the same herd as their mother, even when they too begin to breed. The three young elephants in this group belong to an old cow and her adult daughter.

Young males, or 'bulls', gradually separate from the family when they are between twelve and 20 years old. They then either live alone or join loose-knit **bachelor** herds with other bulls until they are old enough to **breed**. Bachelor herds usually number up to eight animals. Once they reach breeding age, bulls live alone. When bulls want to **mate**, they seek out a herd. At any one time, one-third to one-half of all cow–calf herds are also accompanied by at least one lone bull in search of a mate.

Herd sizes

The great variation in herd size is explained partly by differences in **habitat** and food supply. Prime **floodplain** grassland – grass enriched by the flooding of nearby rivers – in southern India may support up to four elephants per square kilometre, while **tropical** forest in Malaysia may support only one elephant per 70 square kilometres, and therefore much smaller herds. Herds often break down into smaller groups of cow–calf units when there are changes in the environment.

Female leader

Cows may spend their whole life in the herd in which they were born. This means that the eldest herd member is always a female. She is usually between 40 and 60 years old, and her great age has given her a store of knowledge matched by no other herd member. She is known as the **matriarch**. Her skills and her stored memories of where to find food, shelter and water are essential to the herd's survival.

In times of danger the matriarch leads from the front and guides the group to safety. Unfortunately this puts her at most risk of attack from hunters. If a matriarch is shot dead, her herd becomes confused. The members may try to push her body upright again or simply stand about it, trumpeting, unsure of what to do next. For this reason, hunters often shoot deliberately at what they take to be the matriarch. When a matriarch dies of natural causes, herds break down into smaller units of cows and their calves. The next most senior cow may then take over the role of matriarch.

Groups of cows and their calves form a herd at Nagarhole National Park, India. Tigers are now so rare that this is one of the few places where elephants and tigers share living space.

17

On the move

As their diet changes from one season to the next, so elephants move from one food source to another. They also move in response to changing rainfall patterns. This seasonal movement is known as **migration**.

Following the seasons

Elephant expert Dr Raman Sukumar studied an elephant population in the Biligirirangan hills of southern India in 1981–82. He found that during the dry months of January to April, elephants clustered in a forested river valley. It offered shade and a reliable source of water and **browse**.

After the May–August rains, most of the elephants spread out into higher, more open country to graze on tall grasses. With the onset of heavier, **monsoon** rains in September, the animals moved down into areas containing shorter grasses or dry thorn forest, remaining there until December. Shifting food sources are not the only spur for migration. Bush fires force elephants to migrate out of an area, though they often return as soon as green shoots spring from the scorched soil. Biting flies and flooded ground are other annoyances that make elephants move.

▲ *Asian elephants, unlike African elephants, usually travel in single file through woodland, especially where the land is hilly. Their pathways have often been used by many generations of elephants.*

Follow the leader

Some elephant herds move as unpredictably as the weather; others follow traditional routes (and become easy targets for hunters). The herd is led from the front by the **matriarch**. Long experience has taught her where water sources lie, how food sources shift through the year, and so on. This knowledge is passed down from one generation to the next within each herd.

Regional range

Asian elephants are far less given to migrating than their African cousins. In Africa, annual round trips of up to 800 kilometres in Mali and 200 kilometres in Botswana have been observed. A typical seasonal movement in Asia might extend to 20 or 50 kilometres. Differences in the terrain, climate and **vegetation** of the two continents are partly responsible.

Within Asia, elephants migrate in regions where seasonal change is more obvious. In **tropical rainforest**, where seasons do not differ so much, elephants do not need to migrate at certain times of the year. So while elephants regularly move up to 50 kilometres from one feeding site to another in the hills of southern India, they do not migrate at all on the Malay **peninsula**, an area of tropical forest.

No through road

Today, Asian elephants find that traditional migration routes throughout their **range** have been barred by human settlements. This leads to conflict when the animals stray across agricultural land in attempts to follow their traditional 'road map'.

Nose to tail, a herd of elephants follows its female leader into river shallows before spreading out to drink and bathe.

Asian elephant communication

Elephants use smell, sound, gestures and touch to communicate with each other and to detect threats. Their sense of smell is superb, and it is common to see elephants raise their trunks and wave them about in order to home in on a strange scent. Elephants also produce scent, through chemicals in their dung, urine and breath. Each elephant in a herd gets to know the personal scent of all its fellows. This scent awareness comforts calves, reassures adults and strengthens social bonds. Scent plays an important role in **breeding**, too: breeding bulls are especially smelly, and the odour warns non-breeding bulls not to approach them. Scent also helps bulls to detect females that are ready to **mate**.

An elephant raises its trunk. This is a threat display, but it is also a good way of sniffing the air to test another animal's scent and find out whether or not it is friendly.

Calling all elephants

In a forest, however, airborne scent does not travel as far as sound, and elephants use a wide range of calls. These include a deep growl which can be heard by other elephants up to a kilometre away. It is used partly to show contentment but also to say 'I'm over here,' especially when among trees. Elephants trumpet through their trunk when they are excited (such as when greeting relatives), angry, afraid or just playing. A danger alert may be given with a low snort. A dramatic sound is the 'trunk boom', in which an elephant smacks the tip of its trunk on the ground to make an explosively loud sound.

Gestures help an elephant establish its rank in the herd. A high-ranking elephant may carry its head high. A **submissive** animal may place the tip of its trunk into another's mouth. The sensitive tip is very important to an elephant, so placing it where it could be chewed off means trust and surrender. At all times, elephants in a herd love to touch each other, brushing against one another or caressing each other with their trunks.

The trunk is used as a sensitive 'hand' for feeling other animals. Everyday touching helps to strengthen friendships between members of a herd.

How low can they go?

In the 1980s American scientist Dr Katy Payne suggested that deep growling allows elephants to talk in infrasound, a noise that human ears cannot hear. We can hear sounds as low as 20 Hz (hertz, or vibrations per second). Elephants go as low as 14 Hz. Deep notes travel further than high ones. Their infrasonic rumbles may be heard from 8 kilometres away or even more. It explains how separate herds keep in touch when they cannot see one another. Infrasound may also give researchers a way of counting elephant populations. They can leave a microphone and tape recorder in elephant country to record the deep rumbling calls and use computer software to calculate how many animals are present.

Breeding

Elephants live for almost as long as we do, often reaching 60 or 70 years of age. However they do not **breed** in a hurry. A bull is capable of reproducing from about eight years of age, but he rarely does so until he is 20 or even 30 years old. This is because he must compete with other bulls for a **mate**, and to win he must be large and powerful.

When a bull is in 'musth', his cheeks are stained with a fluid that leaks from **glands** *on his head.*

Wandering bulls

Every year a large adult bull comes into a breeding condition known as **'musth'**. The period of musth tends to occur at specific times of the year, depending on the location of the elephants, and lasts for nearly three months.

While in musth, the bull wanders widely in search of mates. If other bulls cross his path, each bull shows off his size and strength by posturing, and by tusking, or thrashing at plants. Their dispute is usually settled without bloodshed – smaller bulls always give way to large bulls, especially those in musth.

Musth madness

'Musth' is a word from India that means 'drunk'. In fact, the bull is affected by a massive surge of the **hormone** testosterone, which floods through his bloodstream at 50 times the normal level. The hormone makes him want to mate, and it also makes him aggressive. The mood changes are a necessary part of the mating process.

Capable cow

For about four days in every 22, a cow is in oestrus. This means she is capable of becoming pregnant. Bulls in musth seek out cows in oestrus to mate with. When a bull has 'won' a cow, he guards her for a day or two and they mate a number of times. He leaves her when her oestrus period ends.

After an average of 646 days – almost two years – a pregnant cow gives birth to a single calf. About 90 centimetres high at the shoulder and weighing over 90 kilograms, it has a coat of reddish or yellowish hair, but this is soon shed.

First steps

The calf is normally on its feet within a couple of hours, seeking its mother's milk. It suckles for a minute or two every 40–50 minutes, day and night, and in every 24 hours the calf drinks up to 15 litres. The calf at first is ungainly and is unsure of how to use its trunk, but the constant company of its mother and play with other calves help it learn as it grows.

From birth onwards, the calf never once leaves its mother's side over the next four years or so. Though it starts to eat **vegetation** at a few months old, it may keep suckling throughout this period. The mother needs endless patience, for she may well have one or two older calves with her. (She may continue to have calves at two- to eight-year intervals until she is in her fifties.) She also has to move more slowly than the rest of the herd. For this reason herds sometimes separate into smaller '**creches**'.

From when it is seven or eight years old, a calf is happy to spend time away from its mother. Its physical growth is still rapid, though at ten years it slows down. At about 30 years of age the elephant has reached full height, though it may continue to gain weight.

A calf uses its mouth, not its trunk, to suckle from its mother, who must stand patiently all the while. You can see the calf's birth coat of hair; it is shed as the animal grows.

Highly intelligent, quick to learn commands and capable of hauling more than half a metric ton, the Asian elephant has long served people in many different roles. More than 5000 years ago, settlers in the Indus Valley of India and Pakistan began taming elephants to help them clear wilderness areas. Over thousands of years, throughout their **range**, tame elephants have been used for many duties: extracting logs from forests, ploughing crops and carrying people and cargo.

Elephants are still used today in parts of Asia to handle heavy burdens. This animal in Delhi, India, is carrying not only its rider, but also its packed lunch!

Royal stables

It became a tradition for nobles and royals to own elephants. Garlanded, painted and jewelled, the animals played a starring role in royal and religious ceremonies, and carried their riders during tiger hunts. Indian rulers set up special reserves where wild elephants were to be captured unharmed. Anyone found killing them was put to death. The populations of the great stables defy belief. The emperor Chandragupta, who ruled India from 321–297 BC, is said to have owned 9000 war elephants.

Elephants at war

Asian elephants served in many ancient battles. In 331 BC, Darius III of Persia set them against the Macedonian leader Alexander the Great. Alexander was so impressed that he used elephants to invade India five years later. The use of war elephants continued in Asia for centuries, though it declined with the widespread introduction of firearms in the 1500s. However, during World War II, the British army had an Elephant Company to help build bridges and haul equipment through the jungles of Burma (now Myanmar). In the Vietnam War (1967–75) US warplanes bombed elephants to stop enemy forces from using the animals as transports. However, elephants were far from ideal in battle. They were nervy and unpredictable, and might suddenly turn on their own men and trample them.

Capture and training

Elephants are not easy to **breed** in captivity, because both sexes need space to roam at will when they are ready to **mate**. In the past it was simpler to capture new animals from the wild population. Early northern Indian peoples caught elephants in a *kheddah*, a timber stockade into which whole herds were driven by men making noise and waving torches. On a good day's hunt 50 or more could be rounded up. Tame elephants were often used in round-ups because of their calming effect on the wild herds. This practice was used across the Asian elephant's range, well into the mid-20th century. Another method involved driving elephants into water and then lassooing them by an ear. Further south, hunters would trap smaller numbers in a large, deep pit.

Elephants can be taught to respond to basic commands within a few days. Usually it takes a week or so to get an elephant to kneel and take its rider, or **mahout**. Elephants may then learn to obey up to a hundred different commands.

In southern India ranks of elephants in colourful dress participate in religious ceremonies. This is the Pooram festival that takes place in Kerala every April.

Religious symbol

The Asian elephant is a sacred figure in Asian religions, and features in ancient Indian myths. Hindus worship the elephant-headed god Ganesh. Ganesh worship has helped protect wild elephants, since Hindus are reluctant to kill them. The elephant has been revered by Buddhists, too, since the third century BC. In their texts the Buddha was reborn as a snow-white elephant with six tusks. Today elephants still play a role in religious festivals.

Losing ground

In spite of its rich history, the Asian elephant has an uncertain future. The greatest threat today is the loss of its **habitat**. India's human population rose from 236 million in 1901 to over one billion in 2003. New people need new land, water and food. Twentieth-century programmes to get rid of **malaria**-carrying mosquitoes in the hills of southern India and the Himalayan foothills have allowed farmers to move in. Across Asia the picture is similar: a rising human population is taking over the remaining wildernesses. One estimate claims that, overall, the Asian elephant has lost up to 70 per cent of its **range** area since the 1960s.

Competing cattle

The ranching of livestock in elephant habitat causes problems. The hooves of cattle compact the soil and stop water from soaking in. Cattle also carry diseases, such as anthrax or foot-and-mouth, which can spread to elephants. Also, where cattle overgraze native plants such as bamboo, weeds are able to invade and take over, reducing the elephants' food supply.

Spreading crops

Deforestation continues today at an alarming rate. **Native vegetation** is giving way to vast **plantations** of export crops such as tea, coffee, sugar cane, cocoa and banana. In southern India about 10 per cent of former elephant country has been lost to plantations of teak and silver oak (both hardwoods used to make furniture), wattle (used in the leather tanning industry), and eucalyptus (used to make plywood and paper pulp, among other things). Malaysia loses over 2 per cent of its forest area each year.

Villagers in Thailand turn a scorched hillside into new crop land. The country, now heavily deforested, offers little habitat to wild elephants and little work for domestic forestry elephants.

Myanmar (Burma) is today one of the few Asian countries that still uses elephants in forestry. Most are put to work handling heavy logs of teak, a timber grown for furniture.

Faster shifting

Much of Asia's moist **tropical** forests are under 'shifting cultivation'. Farmers cut or burn away the forest, then plant a few crops before moving on to a new site. In the farmers' absence, undergrowth is given time to reclaim the **fallow** land, which still provides living space for local elephants. But farmers are being crammed on to ever smaller plots, and are returning sooner to tired land. For example, shifting farmers in southern India once left the land fallow for between ten and 20 years. Today they allow less than five years. As a result, the land becomes unproductive. The elephants have less living space because farmers are leaving less time between planting crops on the same land. This means that there is less time for elephant food plants to grow back.

Uprooted

Logging affects wild animals in many Asian countries. While governments and international associations make attempts to control the extent of deforestation by logging companies, illegal logging continues regardless. Ironically, elephants have been used by loggers for years to clear the very forests they depend upon in the wild.

Asian elephants and farmers

About one-fifth of the world's human population is found in, or very near, Asian elephant **habitat**. Millions of these people are very poor. They will go hungry or even starve if their crops and homes are damaged by elephants. Elephants, forced into ever smaller, isolated clumps of forest, sometimes stray into settlements. Farmers and villagers can come to see elephants as a neighbourhood threat.

*Fields like this coffee **plantation** in Vietnam are no-go areas for elephants. But as more and more land goes under the plough, keeping animals off crops is getting steadily harder.*

Crop raiders

Today, some of the crops elephants raid include millet, banana, rice, sugar cane and oil palm. The elephants feed at night and trample the crops as they eat them. Sometimes a farmer's entire season's crop is destroyed. It is usually mature bulls, either alone or in small groups, that cause the trouble. They wander widely (especially when **breeding**) and are more likely to enter fields. Many bulls develop a taste for crop raiding. Cows tend not to raid crops for fear of putting their calves at risk.

Today, in most **range countries**, it is illegal to kill an elephant without a government licence. Villagers can do little to protect their livelihood, but some take the law into their own hands. During 2001 in Assam in India, villagers poisoned 31 elephants to stop them from crop raiding. In Sri Lanka, an estimated 110–120 elephants are killed each year, mostly after elephants have raided crops.

Why raid crops?

Some elephants raid crops because the fields lie on their ancient **home range**, or because it is the best food available. Plants grown as crops are simply wild plants bred for centuries by humans to be tastier and more **nutritious**. In certain seasons, crops offer elephants more nutrition than wild grasses. Also, crops do not contain the toxins (poisons) produced by wild plants for self-defence against plant-eaters.

Dangerous elephants

Farmers try to shoo raiding elephants away with torches, guns and firecrackers, but bulls are not easily scared, and they can be dangerous too. Up to 150 people are killed by elephants every year in India alone. Many are trampled, gored or hurled aside while trying to protect their crops, but often the victims are presenting no threat. Bulls in **musth**, or **matriarchs** trying to defend their herd, have been known to charge into villages and attack women and children. Sometimes they are simply startled by the bark of a dog.

Keeping elephants at bay

Various methods are tried to protect farmers' fields. Sometimes trenches are dug around crops. A simple soil trench tends to collapse after heavy rain, and elephants are good at crossing them. They simply kick at the top of the slopes until they fill the trench with soil and then cross it. Concrete trenches are too expensive for most farmers to build.

Buffer zones are belts of land that separate elephants from land used by humans. They may be planted with grasses that elephants enjoy, so that the animals eat their fill before they reach crops. Or the zones may be left clear, to deter elephants from crossing them. Buffer zones are only partly effective, and they use up a lot of land.

Another method is to put up an electric fence. This delivers a brief burst of very high voltage. It is very effective, and over a given distance is about one-third the cost of trenching. But electric fences do need maintainance and can be easily stolen by simply taking the wires and battery.

Elephants that keep on raiding crops run the risk of being shot by angry villagers. Some, too, are killed by eating poisoned bait left out for troublesome wild pigs.

Meat and ivory

People **poach** elephants for meat and their skin. The elephant skin is turned into bags and shoes. Skin and meat are both used in Chinese medicine. **Ivory** poaching occurs across the **range**. The trade in Asian elephant ivory is small compared with that in Africa. Asian elephants are fewer in number, harder to track, less likely to carry tusks, and spared by many people for religious reasons. Also, Asian cultures have a much longer tradition of using live elephants in daily life.

In areas where elephants have been raiding crops and damaging buildings, it becomes harder for authorities to control poaching. Villagers are more likely to kill elephants themselves or to support the activities of poachers. If they try to stand up to poachers, they themselves may face death threats. Today's poachers are ruthless, organized gangs with guns. Government **wardens** are hired to combat the gangs, but wardens are costly to hire, and finding people in the forest is like looking for a needle in a haystack.

Ivory trade

Asia plays a key role in the world ivory market. India has a flourishing ivory-carving industry, and for over 2500 years African ivory has been shipped into the country to be carved, then sold on to other parts of the world. Between 1979 and 1990 an estimated 700,000 African elephants – over half the total population – were killed for their tusks. The Asian carving industry grew rapidly to meet the demand.

Looking after its wild cousins: a domestic elephant carries a patrol in search of ivory poachers. The most successful patrols are those that include people with local knowledge.

It is now illegal to sell elephant products between one country and another, but smugglers still try. These customs officials have seized smuggled goods at an Italian airport.

Then in 1990 a world ban on trading in elephant parts, from live animals to elephant products (including teeth, hide, feet, flesh, bones and, of course, ivory) became law. For the thousands of Asian carvers, the supply of legal African ivory ended. So instead many carvers worked on **smuggled** African ivory and newly poached Asian ivory. Some continue to do so today.

Today most western people would rather go without ivory than support this trade. But some markets for ivory are growing. In Japan, for example, ivory *hanko* – personal name stamps – are increasingly popular. In China and the Middle East, too, people are buying more carved ivory than before.

Ban or no ban?

Not all conservationists agree on how best to tackle the ivory trade. Some people think that traders and carvers should be allowed to sell a small amount of ivory each year. Some of the money raised can be channelled to elephant conservation projects. Others argue that this system would be too complicated and give out the wrong message: that it is all right to collect ivory. They say only a total ban will make the public realize that ivory belongs on the elephant and put poachers out of business. Another possibility is to encourage Asia's ivory carvers to work in other materials, such as bone, jade or stone.

Out of balance

Ivory poachers usually target the elephants with the largest tusks – that is to say, mature bulls. The result is that heavily poached populations are running low on mature bulls. It is a particular problem in southern India. The reserves of Bandipur–Mudumalai contain one bull to every 12 to 15 cows, while the Periyar Tiger Reserve contains one to every hundred. With so few bulls, **breeding** is slowed and populations start to tumble.

It is not just wild elephants that are losing the fight for survival. There are also threats facing tame elephants, which make up as much as a third of the total Asian elephant population.

Why keep elephants today?

In all countries where elephants live in the wild, except in Myanmar (Burma), capturing elephants is now illegal (it was banned in India in 1973), and there are strict controls on forestry. However in small numbers elephants still fulfil a variety of roles. Some countries, such as India and Myanmar, still use their tame elephants for **logging**, since the animals can work in mountains where vehicles cannot go.

Tourists in Royal Chitwan National Park, Nepal, take an elephant ride to view an even rarer native: the one-horned rhinoceros.

Many elephants are still used in entertainment and tourism, though they are closely monitored by animal rights campaigners. In India, for example, elephants are kept in zoos, perform in circuses and are kept in private collections, some of which use their animals as tourist attractions.

Currently fewer than half of India's captive elephants are registered on ownership certificates. Efforts are underway to have all elephant owners register their animals with the authorities. The information, stored on computers, will enable conservationists to manage populations, keep accurate counts, and monitor any cases of animal abuse.

Out-of-work elephants

A decline in the forestry industry has meant less work for tame elephants. Many elephants that were once busy in the timber camps are now out of work. Thailand, for example, has lost about three-quarters of its forest area since 1900. The country's captive elephant population has fallen from over 13,000 in 1950 to 4000 today. Thailand banned the use of elephants in logging in 1989, and now these few animals are mostly out of work. Desperate keepers earned money by making their elephants perform tricks for tourists in cities such as Bangkok. The elephants were poorly cared for. In 2002, after worldwide public outrage, the Thai government banned elephants from cities. This has merely shifted the problem. The 'unemployed' elephants are now led by their **mahouts** around the back roads and tourist sites to beg for handouts.

An Asian keeper traditionally hobbles his elephant with chains to keep it from wandering and to make it easier to handle. Many people now feel that this method of restraint is cruel.

Hard to handle

Elephants are difficult to maintain. Until recent decades keepers could expect to lose up to half of their elephants in the first week of captivity. A common cause of death was a 'broken heart' – a rather poetic term for overworked heart muscles. When their bulls came into **musth** and became hard to restrain, the more ignorant keepers would shackle their feet and give them powerful drugs or poisons, often killing them. As late as the 20th century, vets were still recommending the drug opium, or poisons like arsenic and strychnine, for medicinal use.

Health problems are a key issue as the world's captive Asian elephant population enters old age. Even today, with modern medicine, tame elephants suffer foot and skin infections if they are not exercised and groomed regularly. Without a proper diet they suffer vitamin deficiency. They need space to roam and the company of others.

The zoo debate

An elephant in an Alaska zoo with its keeper. Weather conditions like this are far from ideal for an animal that is used to hot climates.

Keeping large mammals in zoos is never easy. Visitors to modern zoos want to see animals kept in conditions as near to natural as possible. But a report on European zoos published in 2002 revealed that elephants are still being mistreated. For example the report found that herds in zoos are too small. Cows are kept apart – sometimes permanently – from their calves and sisters. Even the best enclosures are up to a hundred times smaller than **home ranges** in the wild. Elephants are still tied with leg chains for several hours a day.

Zoo elephants often suffer from health problems. Because of the cold, wet weather in **temperate** countries, elephants there may be kept indoors for up to sixteen hours a day. The lack of exercise and an unbalanced diet mean that cows are up to 70 per cent heavier than their wild counterparts. Damp conditions and hard floors lead to the early onset of **arthritis**. Some 40 per cent of zoo elephants show some form of what is called 'stereotypic behaviour' – for example, treading the same path again and again, or endlessly weaving the head from side to side. It is no surprise then that an Asian elephant's average lifespan in a zoo is only fifteen years.

Number of registered captive Asian elephants

The International Species Information System (ISIS), an international non-profit organization, and the Captive Elephant Database (CED), run by elephant keepers, both list the animals kept in zoos and similar institutions. These numbers do not include thousands of unregistered tame elephants.

Continent	Zoos & safari parks	Circuses	Working camps & private owners
Europe	330	184	0
North and Central America	210	184	14
Asia	79+	11	8
Africa	5+	3	0
Australia	10	9	0
South America	0+	0	0
World total	**634+**	**391**	**22**

Why keep elephants in zoos?

The managers of zoos claim that keeping elephants offers many benefits, including better elephant research. Biologists can study the elephants at close quarters. By claiming that the elephants are for 'research' purposes, zoos can obtain a rare legal permit to **import** elephants. Zoo supporters also point to the fact that admission charges from zoo visitors help pay for conservation schemes in the elephants' **range countries**. Watching elephants close up allows us to learn more about them, and stirs our interest in conservation. Matching **breeding** pairs allows conservationists to sustain **genetic diversity** and breed animals to be reintroduced into the wild.

Opponents of zoos counter these claims. Though zoo elephants are certainly useful, biologists could also study orphans or working elephants in **logging** camps. Elephants are actually very expensive to house in zoos, and this cost must be set against the amount of money they raise in admission charges. People don't need to see captive elephants in order to be persuaded to make donations. There is little educational value to be had from seeing poorly kept or ill elephants. Furthermore elephants do not breed well in captivity. It is 50 times cheaper to manage herds in the wild than to keep similar numbers in zoos.

As wild herds dwindle and the captive population becomes increasingly significant, the debate over keeping elephants in zoos looks set to continue.

It's thrilling for zoo visitors but is it good for the elephant? Modern zoos such as London Zoo try to keep their animals in pens that are as close as possible to conditions in the wild.

Because there are many different threats to the Asian elephant, conservation needs action on many fronts.

Elephants and the law

The Asian elephant is on Appendix I to CITES, the Convention on International Trade in Endangered **Species** of Wild Fauna and Flora. Any animal listed on Appendix I cannot be traded internationally without a special licence. The Asian elephant was among the first animals on Appendix I when CITES came into being in 1975. One of the most important laws protecting elephants in India is the Wildlife Act, first introduced in 1972. Following the elephant's listing on CITES, India has upgraded the 1972 act several times. In 1978, for example, it banned export of the Asian elephant, and in 1986 it banned the ivory trade within India. Another milestone law was the ban on the international trade in ivory. Since it came into effect in 1990 the ban has helped stabilize elephant numbers in both Africa and Asia. In 1997 the United States passed the Asian Elephant Conservation Act, and has since donated several million dollars to more than 40 different elephant conservation projects.

Conserving habitat

Currently, of the 440,000 square kilometres where Asian elephants still live, only 130,000 square kilometres – or one-third – lie within reserves or sanctuaries. Though these areas are still targeted by **poachers** and illegal **loggers** or farmers, some protection is better than no protection. About 2000 Asian elephants live in India's Kaziranga National Park and the Nagaland hills. In southern India, over 1100 Asian elephants live in the Periyar Tiger Reserve. At Periyar, and in the Nagarhole National Park, Bandipur Tiger Reserve and Mudumalai Sanctuary in the Nilgiri hills, there are one to three elephants per square kilometre.

A calf feeds from its mother in the Kaziranga National Park, India, one of several sites where the WWF is helping to conserve elephants.

In Thailand there are four major protected areas for elephants. Khao Yai National Park is home to about 225 elephants. The existing protected area covers some 25,000 square kilometres but is home to only 50 per cent of the wild elephants that live in the country. Chinese elephants are confined to the **tropical** forests of the Xishuangbanna Nature Reserve, in Yunnan province.

Flagships

Increasingly, governments and conservation organizations are focusing their work on preserving areas that are especially rich in plants and animals. It helps, too, when such hotspots contain 'flagship' animals, such as elephants, tigers or rhinoceroses that have strong support from local residents and the wider public. Protecting a flagship species is a very effective way of saving a wildlife hotspot from destruction.

Corridors

To link isolated elephant populations, conservationists create 'green corridors' of elephant-friendly terrain between key **habitat** areas. In Thailand, for example, the Royal Forest Department is working with local people to create a 700-metre corridor between two protected areas, the Ang Luenai Wildlife Sanctuary and Khao Chamao National Park. It is a situation that helps everyone: the elephants get living space, while the local farmers keep their crops elephant-free. The World Land Trust has also begun a project to link protected areas in north-east India with three corridors. The Siju-Rewak elephant corridor will put about 20 per cent of the world's Asian elephants (around 9200 animals) in contact with each other.

The WWF and AREAS

The Worldwide Fund for Nature (WWF) is currently running an Asian Rhino and Elephant Area Strategy (AREAS). The AREAS programme has identified eight elephant 'priority landscapes' spread over seven **range countries**. WWF is trying to establish new national parks and reserves in the priority landscapes, promote better use of natural resources, and improve anti-poaching measures. Many other rare **mammals** are likely to benefit from AREAS, including the tiger, sun bear, sloth bear, clouded leopard and Ganges river dolphin.

WWF's elephant priority landscapes:

India	Nilgiris/Eastern Ghats
	Kaziranga/Karbi-Anglong
	Arunachal/Assam/Namdapha
Thailand	Tenasserim/
	Western Forest Complex
Malaysia/Indonesia	south Sabah/
	north-east Kalimantan
Malaysia/Thailand	Hala Bala National Park/
	Taman Negara National Park
Indonesia	Tesso Nilo
Vietnam/Laos/Cambodia	Emerald Triangle

The plight of Sumatran elephants shows how the conflict between elephants and locals is placing a growing burden on governments. **Tropical** lowland **rainforest** once covered almost all of Sumatra, one of the largest Indonesian islands. In some places swampy and in others mountainous, the forest provided a vast **habitat** for the island's orangutans, tigers, rhinos and elephants. After World War II, the government began moving millions of Indonesian people from the heavily overcrowded islands of Java, Bali and Madera to Sumatra and other islands. Since then, forest has been cleared to make way for the settlers and their crops, which include rice, rubber and coffee.

There has also been a rapid growth of commercial **logging** and farming on Sumatra over the last 50 years. Much of the logging is illegal and almost impossible for the authorities to control. **Plantations** of oil palms and softwood trees are replacing the forest so rapidly that it is feared the island will lose all of its lowland rainforest by 2010. New roads, oil and gas wells, mines and forest fires only add to the threats facing Sumatra's remaining wild places.

As elephant habitat on Sumatra is slashed to make way for crop plantations, 'refugees' like these are flooding the island's rescue centres, which simply cannot cope with the high numbers.

Elephant threats

This loss of habitat has splintered the Sumatran elephant's populations. By the 1990s there were an estimated 44 separate populations. Only fifteen of these were thought to contain more than a hundred elephants. Elephants are being forced into new and unfamiliar **ranges**, alarming local people. Fishermen, for example, have been setting spear traps and shooting or poisoning elephants simply because they do not want the animals around. Other elephants have been made homeless by the relentless clearance of forest.

Rescue centres

The Indonesian government rescues Sumatran elephants that have been made homeless or threatened with persecution by locals. Since the 1980s it has been trying to transfer them from problem areas to wildernesses, but suitable habitat is fast running out. In the meantime, rescue animals are housed in special 'camps'. In 1991–2001 alone, 500 elephants were taken into centres on the island. But many of the centres cannot afford to care for their animals or the environment.

For example, a survey in 2000 found that the Sebanga-Duri Centre in Riau, Sumatra, had a monthly veterinary budget of only one US dollar per elephant, a figure far short of what is required. Most of the elephants were sickening from an unbalanced diet and poisonous drinking water. Farmers, loggers and oil palm planters had illegally taken over 80 per cent of the centre's original land area.

In an attempt to cut the costs of running the centres, the government is asking tourist operators, logging companies, zoos and conservation centres to take the rescue elephants. So far they have managed to rehouse more than 250 animals. But overall the programme has not been a great success. Like the government, private companies find elephant keeping too expensive.

The Sumatran elephant is also known as the 'pocket elephant' because it is smaller than most other subspecies. Sadly, its forest habitat now survives only in small pockets.

About half of the Asian elephant's remaining **range** is likely to be lost by 2050 unless action is taken. It is up to governments to clamp down on illegal **loggers** and **plantation** owners, and to research non-destructive ways of exploiting forests.

Creating new reserves and linking corridors, as well as strengthening protection of existing areas, is essential. But with so many rural people in desperate need of natural **resources**, it is wrong to put the elephants' needs first. The challenge is to find solutions that benefit both elephants and people. These include, for example, moving bulls from where they are causing problems and introducing them to herds that need mature bulls. Also, captives all over the world could be used as **gene** 'banks', to be introduced into wild herds before individuals become too closely related to each other.

*Crop-raiders and other troublesome elephants can be moved. This **tranquillized** elephant is being nudged into a truck by domestic elephants, which also have a calming effect on the wild animal.*

New homes for troublemakers

Translocation involves taking a particularly troublesome elephant from a conflict zone and moving it to new **habitat**. It is an expensive method, involving fencing, wardening and the creation of special corridors of land. Often the elephant does not settle in its new home and tries to leave – but the scheme can work. Sugar cane planters on Sumatra successfully drove an entire herd of 70 elephants from crop land to a nearby game reserve in 1984–85.

Turning poachers into protectors

In many regions there is a strong link between villagers and **poachers**. Villagers who have suffered from elephant raids are quite happy for poachers to remove what they see as the cause of their misfortune.

One way to break this link is to pay villagers **compensation** money for lost crops or family members killed by elephants. This requires a great deal of organization, and sometimes a government cannot afford to pay. In the Xishuangbanna reserve in China, for example, a tiny elephant population – fewer than 200 – caused £1.5 million worth of damage to crops and rubber trees during 2001. That year, however, the government had a total fund of only £63,453 to hand out.

Another way to involve locals in the fight against poaching is to train them to work as anti-poaching **wardens**. That way, they are paid to protect what will come to be seen as their natural heritage. Local people can also find work as rangers, tour guides and research assistants.

Schoolchildren in Sri Lanka pay a visit to an elephant orphanage. An experience like this can teach young people that their natural heritage is worth saving.

Creating a caring generation

None of these changes will succeed without teaching people to care about elephants. For example, in India, the Centre for Environment Education has designed workbooks for pupils, and posters and handbooks for teachers that help 10–14-year-old pupils learn about the Asian elephant. The package is being sent to hundreds of schools in India, Sri Lanka and Bangladesh.

What can you do?

It might seem that unless you live in one of its **range countries**, you can do nothing to save the Asian elephant. But there are ways you can affect how people treat the environment in Asia.

Save the forests

Saving Asian forests can help save elephants – not to mention orangutans, rhinos, proboscis monkeys and other rare animals. The United Kingdom **imports** more illegally harvested Indonesian timber than does any other European country. Write to your Member of Parliament asking him or her to push for tighter control over timber imports. The United States imports about $450 million (£300 million) worth of timber from Indonesia. A significant amount of this is illegally harvested, then **smuggled** to the USA by way of Singapore.

Ask your parents to make sure they buy products – picture frames and wooden furniture, for example – made from legally harvested timber. Shopkeepers should be able to explain where they get their stock from and to assure customers that it is legal. If your parents buy timber for DIY jobs, they should look for the green Forest Stewardship Council (FSC) logo on the timber; this shows that the timber comes from a managed forest. The FSC is an international timber watchdog based in Oaxaca, Mexico.

A tiny orphan elephant at Kaziranga National Park. It was rescued by the Wildlife Trust of India, a partner of the IFAW.

Join a support group

There are many conservation organizations worldwide helping to save both Asian and African elephants. Most of them are charity-based: they depend on people giving them money to support their activities. When you pay a subscription fee to join a charity that supports elephant conservation projects, you are contributing to their funds. You can also help raise funds by organizing an awareness event for the charity of your choice.

Live on TV!
The Elephant Sanctuary is a home for sick and needy Asian elephants based on a ranch near Nashville, Tennessee, USA. You can watch the resident animals on a live webcam.

Kuala Gandah in Malaysia is one of many field centres in Asia working to save the elephant. Their first step is to raise money and public awareness.

There are plenty of organizations to choose from. The IFAW (International Fund for Animal Welfare) has an Asian and African elephant campaign. The Elephant Family brings together experts in Asian elephant biology and conservation in a range of field projects in the elephants' range countries. Friends of the Asian Elephant is concerned with the welfare of Thailand's elephants. The Elephant Help Project is another Thai elephant conservation programme. The Malaysian Elephant Appeal funds the care of animals held at the Kuala Gandah Elephant Centre, Malaysia.

IFAW

INTERNATIONAL FUND FOR ANIMAL WELFARE
WWW.IFAW.ORG

Glossary

arthritis painful swelling of the body's joints

bachelor single male

breed produce offspring (babies)

browse foliage and woody material, especially twigs and bark, from plants; also to eat such material

circumference length of the line that forms a circle

compensate repay someone for a loss or injury

creche where young are kept in a group and cared for by a few adults

deforestation destruction of a forest

digestion process where food that has been eaten is broken down in the stomach and intestines and the body takes the nutrients it needs

DNA (deoxyribonucleic acid), a chemical inside cells that forms instructions called genes, telling cells how to work and grow

evaporate turn from liquid into vapour

fallow land that is left unplanted after a crop has been harvested there

floodplain riverside area that is regularly drenched or flooded by the river; typically rich in nutrients deposited from the water

genes tiny units of an animal cell that are arranged differently in every living thing; the order in which they are arranged is what makes each individual unique. Genes are passed on from parent to baby.

genetic diversity when individuals in a group have inherited different genes

germinate when a seed sprouts and begins to grow

gland body organ that releases a particular substance that helps the body work

gut stomach and canal through which food passes in order to be digested

habitat animal's natural living space

home range area within which an animal lives and which supplies all the animal's needs

hormone chemical in the body that can affect mood and health

humid damp

import bring in from another country

ivory hard, creamy-white substance making up most of an elephant's tusk

logging harvesting trees for commercial use

mahout Hindi word for trained elephant rider and keeper

malaria disease in humans carried by mosquitoes; causes fever and can kill

mammal warm-blooded animal that feeds its young on milk from the mother's body

mate when two animals get together to produce offspring; also a partner with which an animal can produce offspring

matriarch female who is accepted as leader of the herd because of her great age and experience

migration   regular seasonal movement of an animal, usually made across land or up and down hills

molar   cheek tooth, usually with a ridged crown (top) for grinding food

monsoon   seasonal wind in Asia that brings heavy rainfall; also describes rainy season itself

musth   condition in which a bull elephant's body prepares for mating and his behaviour becomes more excitable and aggressive

native   belonging to a specified place; one who belongs to that place

nutritious   food that contains chemicals that help a body grow and function

organisms   living bodies

peninsula   long piece of land that sticks out like a finger into a sea or ocean

plantation   large field containing a single crop planted in lines or rows

poacher   person who illegally kills and takes an animal or part of an animal (i.e. an elephant's tusks)

predator   animal that hunts and kills other animals

prehistoric   time before humans started leaving a record of their existence

radio transmitter   device that sends out a radio signal

rainforest   leafy forest that grows wherever annual rainfall is higher than 2500 millimetres

range   overall area where a wildlife species is found

range countries   countries where elephants live

resources   things that can be useful

satellite   spacecraft circling Earth; some are used to bounce radio signals from one place to another

scrub   rough terrain dotted with stunted clumps of plant life

smuggle   carry or move something that you are not allowed to carry

species   scientific name for a particular kind of plant, animal or other living thing. Two individuals of the same species can reproduce and have babies. Individuals from separate species cannot.

submissive   accepting a lower rank than another member of one's own group

temperate   climate that features winters and summers without extremes of temperature

thicket   area of overgrown shrubs

tranquillize   make calm, stable or unconscious with the use of chemicals

tropical   being found on or near the equator, an imaginary line running around the planet at an equal distance between the north and south poles. Tropical areas have a moist and very warm climate.

vegetation   plants

warden   person who is employed to protect a place or an animal

Useful contacts and further reading

Websites

Elephanteria
www.himandus.net/elephanteria/
Elephanteria is full of information on both African and Asian elephants.
It also tells you how to make elephant masks, elephant breakfasts,
elephant flags and stickers.

The Malaysian Elephant Satellite Tracking Project
www.hrw.com/science/si-science/biology/animals/elephant/elenewex.html
A joint American–Malaysian educational presentation; it features a
classroom debate based on a conflict over elephants, agriculture and
the needs of local people.

WWF
www.worldwildlife.org/areas/
Find out more about WWF's elephant projects in southeastern Asia.

Animal Defenders
www.ad-international.org
The many campaigns of this UK-based organization include a petition
to end the use and abuse of animals in captivity, with specific
attention to the plight of circus elephants.

IFAW
www.ifaw.org
The International Fund for Animal Welfare has an Asian and African
elephant campaign.

Elephant Family
www.elephantfamily.org
Organizes field projects in Asian elephant range countries.

Friends of the Asian Elephant
www.elephant.tnet.co.th/index_21.1.html
Looks after the welfare of Thailand's Asian elephants.

The Elephant Help Project
www.elephanthelp.org
Another Thai conservation programme.

The Elephant Sanctuary

www.elephants.com

A home for sick and needy elephants in Tennessee, USA. Watch the animals on a live webcam.

The Malaysian Elephant Appeal

www.elephantappeal.org

Funds the care of animals held at the Kuala Gandah Elephant Centre in Malaysia.

Books

Animal Groups: Life in a Herd – Elephants, Richard and Louise Spilsbury (Heinemann Library, 2004)

Elephants, Patricia Kendel (Hodder Children's Books, 2002)

Elephants, Ian Redmond (Dorling Kindersley, 2000)

The Elephant Hospital, Kathy Darling (Millbrook Press, 2002)

Hansa: The True Story of an Asian Elephant Baby, Clare Hodgson Meeker (Sasquatch Books, 2002)

In the Forest with Elephants, Roland Smith, Michael J. Schmidt, ed. Anne Davies (Gulliver Green, 1998)

Silent Thunder: The Hidden Voice of Elephants, Katy Payne (Phoenix, 1999)

Travels with Tarra, Carol Buckley (Tilbury House Publishers, 2002)

Index

Titles in the *Animals under Threat* series include:

Hardback   0 431 18902 1

Hardback   0 431 18903 X

Hardback   0 431 18904 8

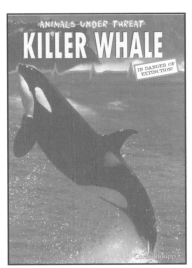

Hardback   0 431 18905 6

Hardback   0 431 18906 4

Hardback   0 431 18907 2

Find out about the other titles in this series on our website www.heinemann.co.uk/library